I0148857

Cool Ships
USS Chosin CG 65
US Navy Guided Missile Cruiser

W. Frederick Zimmerman

Copyright © 2020 Frederick Zimmerman

All rights reserved.

ISBN: 9781608880911

DEDICATION

To the ships and sailors of the U.S. Navy past, present, and future.

CONTENTS

ACKNOWLEDGMENTS

Thank you to the staff of the Defense Visual Information Distribution System and military photographers everywhere.

OUTSTANDING PHOTOGRAPH

The Nimble Award for Outstanding Photograph of this ship goes to Public Affairs Officer Peter Walz for this memorable photograph of *Chosin* entering Sydney Harbor.

U.S. Navy sailors assigned to USS Chosin (CG 65) prepare the anchor detail as they pull into Sydney harbor to join 40 other military ships and 17 historic tall ships as part of the International Fleet Review - the 100th anniversary celebration of the Royal Australian Navy into Sydney. Military forces from nearly 20 nations are participating in the events which will include public ship tours, fleet parade, and fireworks light show. Chosin is currently operating in the 7th Fleet area of responsibility conducting exercises, port visits, and operations to enhance maritime partnerships and promote peace and stability in the Indo-Asia-Pacific region. (U.S. Navy photo by Public Affairs Officer Peter Walz)

OUTSTANDING NATIONAL SERVICE

The Nimble Award for Outstanding National Service goes to the crew of *Chosin* for the spirit exemplified by this photograph.

With a fully dressed ship and streamers, U.S. Navy sailors assigned to USS Chosin (CG 65) man the rails as they await the pass and review in Sydney harbor. The crew is participating with 20 other global navies as part of the International Fleet Review - the 100th anniversary celebration of the Royal Australian Navy into Sydney. Chosin is currently operating in the 7th Fleet area of responsibility conducting exercises, port visits, and operations to enhance maritime partnerships and promote peace and stability in the Indo-Asia-Pacific region. (U.S. Navy photo by Public Affairs Officer Peter Walz)

IMAGES

U.S. Navy sailors assigned to USS Chosin along with Navy personnel representing 11 other nations are ferried from their mother ships to HMAS Creswell to attend a briefing focused on, ADMM+, ASEAN Defense Ministers Meeting Plus, a major multi-lateral activity to promote practical Maritime cooperation and information sharing among participating Indo-Asian-Pacific countries and to build a common understanding of interoperability procedures in Maritime Security matters. US Navy sailors assigned to USS Chosin are participating in combined navies exercises and an International Fleet Review in Sydney from Sept. 29 through Oct. 18. US Navy photo by Public Affairs Officer Peter Walz

A Japanese Naval officer looks back at Chief Petty Officers Matt Mistove and William Kalmbach as they are ferried from their mother ships to HMAS Creswell to attend a briefing focused on, ADMM+, ASEAN Defense Ministers Meeting Plus, a major multi-lateral activity to promote practical Maritime cooperation and information sharing among participating Indo-Asian-Pacific countries and to build a common understanding of interoperability procedures in Maritime Security matters. U.S. Navy sailors assigned to USS Chosin are participating in combined navies exercises and an International Fleet Review in Sydney from Sept. 29 through Oct. 18. US Navy photo by Public Affairs Officer Peter Walz

U.S. Navy sailors assigned to USS Chosin along with Navy personnel representing 11 other nations attend a briefing focused on, ADMM+, ASEAN Defense Ministers Meeting Plus, a major multi-lateral activity to promote practical Maritime cooperation and information sharing among participating Indo-Asian-Pacific countries and to build a common understanding of interoperability procedures in Maritime Security matters. US Navy sailors assigned to USS Chosin are participating in combined navies exercises and an International Fleet Review in Sydney from Sept. 29 through Oct. 18. US Navy photo by Public Affairs Officer Peter Walz

Lt. j.g. Kenneth Lee assigned to USS Chosin speaks wtih Japanese and Chinese Naval officers as they are ferried from their mother ships to HMAS Creswell to attend a briefing focused on, ADMM+, ASEAN Defense Ministers Meeting Plus, a major multi-lateral activity to promote practical Maritime cooperation and information sharing among participating Indo-Asian-Pacific countries and to build a common understanding of interoperability procedures in Maritime Security matters. US Navy sailors assigned to USS Chosin are participating in combined navies exercises and an International Fleet Review in Sydney from Sept. 29 through Oct. 18. US Navy photo by Public Affairs Officer Peter Walz

Lt. j.g. Kenneth Lee and Ensign Kara VanSice assigned to USS Chosin are ferried to HMAS Creswell to attend a briefing focused on, ADMM+, ASEAN Defense Ministers Meeting Plus, a major multi-lateral activity to promote practical Maritime cooperation and information sharing among participating Indo-Asian-Pacific countries and to build a common understanding of interoperability procedures in Maritime Security matters. US Navy sailors assigned to USS Chosin are participating in combined navies exercises and an International Fleet Review in Sydney from Sept. 29 through Oct. 18. US Navy photo by Public Affairs Officer Peter Walz

U.S. Navy sailors assigned to USS Chosin are participating in combined navies exercises and an International Fleet Review in Sydney from Sept. 29 through Oct. 18. The fleet training exercise dubbed, ADMM+, ASEAN Defense Ministers Meeting Plus, is a major multi-lateral activity to promote practical Maritime cooperation and information sharing among participating Indo-Asian-Pacific countries and to build a common understanding of interoperability procedures in Maritime Security matters. US Navy photo by Public Affairs Officer Peter Walz

Boatswain's Mate Petty Officer 3rd Class (SW) Susana Espinosa and Seaman Courtney Privott assigned to USS Chosin setup the pilot's ladder to transfer personnel to a smaller boat. The crew is participating in combined navies exercises and an International Fleet Review in Sydney from Sept. 29 through Oct. 18. The fleet training exercise dubbed, ADMM+, ASEAN Defense Ministers Meeting Plus, is a major multi-lateral activity to promote practical Maritime cooperation and information sharing among participating Indo-Asian-Pacific countries and to build a common understanding of interoperability procedures in Maritime Security matters. US Navy photo by Public Affairs Officer Peter Walz

Executive Officer of USS Chosin, Cmdr. Troy Fendrick, and Lt. Cmdr. Gavin Telford of the Royal Australian Navy Reserve prepare to board a small ferry vessel headed to HMAS Creswell to attend a briefing focused on, ADMM+, ASEAN Defense Ministers Meeting Plus, a major multi-lateral activity to promote practical Maritime cooperation and information sharing among participating Indo-Asian-Pacific countries and to build a common understanding of interoperability procedures in Maritime Security matters. US Navy sailors assigned to USS Chosin are participating in combined navies exercises and an International Fleet Review in Sydney from Sept. 29 through Oct. 18. US Navy photo by Public Affairs Officer Peter Walz

Boatswain's Mate Petty Officer 3rd Class (SW) Susana Espinosa and Seaman Courtney Privott assigned to USS Chosin setup the pilot's ladder to transfer personnel to a smaller boat. The crew is participating in combined navies exercises and an International Fleet Review in Sydney from Sept. 29 through Oct. 18. The fleet training exercise dubbed, ADMM+, ASEAN Defense Ministers Meeting Plus, is a major multi-lateral activity to promote practical Maritime cooperation and information sharing among participating Indo-Asian-Pacific countries and to build a common understanding of interoperability procedures in Maritime Security matters. US Navy photo by Public Affairs Officer Peter Walz

Chief Petty Officer Anissa Eversley oversees a small boat transfer from the deck of USS Chosin. The small boat ferried US Navy personnel and members of 11 participating navies to a briefing as part of a fleet training exercise dubbed, ADMM+, ASEAN Defense Ministers Meeting Plus, a major multi-lateral activity to promote practical Maritime cooperation and information sharing among participating Indo-Asian-Pacific countries and to build a common understanding of interoperability procedures in Maritime Security matters. US Navy photo by Public Affairs Officer Peter Walz

Aboard the Japanese warship Makanami, Chief Petty Officer Matt Mistove and Lt. j.g. Kenneth Lee listen to and observe an Indonesian boarding officer as he briefs one of the boarding teams who participated in the exercise. U.S. Navy personnel from USS Chosin are participating in combined navies exercises and an International Fleet Review in Sydney Sept. 29 through Oct. 18. The fleet training exercise dubbed ADMM+, ASEAN Defense Ministers Meeting Plus, is a major multi-lateral activity to promote practical Maritime cooperation and information sharing among participating Indo-Asian-Pacific countries and to build a common understanding of interoperability procedures in maritime security matters. (U.S. Navy photo by Public Affairs Officer Peter Walz)

Aboard the Japanese warship Makanami, Chief Petty Officer Matt Mistove and Lt. j.g. Kenneth Lee listen to and observe an Indonesian boarding officer as he briefs one of the boarding teams who participated in the exercise. U.S. Navy personnel from USS Chosin are participating in combined navies exercises and an International Fleet Review in Sydney Sept. 29 through Oct. 18. The fleet training exercise dubbed ADMM+, ASEAN Defense Ministers Meeting Plus, is a major multi-lateral activity to promote practical Maritime cooperation and information sharing among participating Indo-Asian-Pacific countries and to build a common understanding of interoperability procedures in maritime security matters. (U.S. Navy photo by Public Affairs Officer Peter Walz)

Aboard the Japanese warship Makanami, Chief Petty Officer Matt Mistove and Lt. j.g. Kenneth Lee listen to and observe an Indonesian boarding officer as he briefs one of the boarding teams who participated in the exercise. U.S. Navy personnel from USS Chosin are participating in combined navies exercises and an International Fleet Review in Sydney Sept. 29 through Oct. 18. The fleet training exercise dubbed ADMM+, ASEAN Defense Ministers Meeting Plus, is a major multi-lateral activity to promote practical Maritime cooperation and information sharing among participating Indo-Asian-Pacific countries and to build a common understanding of interoperability procedures in maritime security matters. (U.S. Navy photo by Public Affairs Officer Peter Walz)

Left to right, Petty Officer 2nd Class Paul Salas and Petty Officer 1st Class Matthew Fredrickson of USS Chosin navigate a rigid-hulled inflatable boat toward the Japanese military ship Makinami to observe ship-boarding exercises. The fleet training exercise dubbed ADMM+, ASEAN Defense Ministers Meeting Plus, is a major multi-lateral activity to promote practical maritime cooperation and information sharing among participating Indo-Asian-Pacific countries and to build a common understanding of interoperability procedures in maritime security matters. The crew of USS Chosin is participating in combined navies exercises and an International Fleet Review in Sydney Sept. 29 through Oct. 18. (U.S. Navy photo by Public Affairs Officer Peter Walz)

Left to right, Petty Officer 2nd Class Paul Salas and Petty Officer 1st Class Matthew Fredrickson of USS Chosin navigate a rigid-hulled inflatable boat toward the Japanese military ship Makinami to observe ship-boarding exercises. The fleet training exercise dubbed ADMM+, ASEAN Defense Ministers Meeting Plus, is a major multi-lateral activity to promote practical maritime cooperation and information sharing among participating Indo-Asian-Pacific countries and to build a common understanding of interoperability procedures in maritime security matters. The crew of USS Chosin is participating in combined navies exercises and an International Fleet Review in Sydney Sept. 29 through Oct. 18. (U.S. Navy photo by Public Affairs Officer Peter Walz)

Left to right, Petty Officer 2nd Class Paul Salas, Petty Officer 1st Class Matthew Fredrickson, and Ensign John Boyle of USS Chosin navigate a rigid-hulled inflatable boat toward the Japanese military ship Makinami to observe ship-boarding exercises. The fleet training exercise dubbed ADMM+, ASEAN Defense Ministers Meeting Plus, is a major multi-lateral activity to promote practical maritime cooperation and information sharing among participating Indo-Asian-Pacific countries and to build a common understanding of interoperability procedures in maritime security matters. The crew of USS Chosin is participating in combined navies exercises and an International Fleet Review in Sydney Sept. 29 through Oct. 18. (U.S. Navy photo by Public Affairs Officer Peter Walz)

U.S. Navy sailors assigned to USS Chosin greet naval personnel from India and New Zealand as part of the fleet training exercise dubbed ADMM+, ASEAN Defense Ministers Meeting Plus, a major multi-lateral activity to promote practical maritime cooperation and information sharing among participating Indo-Asian-Pacific countries and to build a common understanding of interoperability procedures in maritime security matters. U.S. Navy sailors assigned to USS Chosin are participating in combined navies exercises and an International Fleet Review in Sydney Sept. 29 through Oct. 18. (U.S. Navy photo by Public Affairs Officer Peter Walz)

Chief Petty Officer Matt Mistove assigned to USS Chosin greets naval personnel from Japan and Australia as part of the fleet training exercise dubbed ADMM+, ASEAN Defense Ministers Meeting Plus, a major multi-lateral activity to promote practical maritime cooperation and information sharing among participating Indo-Asian-Pacific countries and to build a common understanding of interoperability procedures in maritime security matters. U.S. Navy sailors assigned to USS Chosin are participating in combined navies exercises and an International Fleet Review in Sydney Sept. 29 through Oct. 18. (U.S. Navy photo by Public Affairs Officer Peter Walz)

U.S. Navy sailor Lt. j.g. Kenneth Lee assigned to USS Chosin watches a boarding exercise between naval personnel from India and New Zealand. The fleet training exercise dubbed ADMM+, ASEAN Defense Ministers Meeting Plus, is a major multi-lateral activity to promote practical maritime cooperation and information sharing among participating Indo-Asian-Pacific countries and to build a common understanding of interoperability procedures in maritime security matters. U.S. Navy sailors assigned to USS Chosin are participating in combined navies exercises and an International Fleet Review in Sydney Sept. 29 through Oct. 18. (U.S. Navy photo by Public Affairs Officer Peter Walz)

With a fully dressed ship and streamers, Chief Petty Officer Matt Mistove and other sailors assigned to USS Chosin (CG 65) man the rails as they await the pass and review in Sydney harbor. The crew is participating with 20 other global navies as part of the International Fleet Review - the 100th anniversary celebration of the Royal Australian Navy into Sydney. Chosin is currently operating in the 7th Fleet area of responsibility conducting exercises, port visits, and operations to enhance maritime partnerships and promote peace and stability in the Indo-Asia-Pacific region. (U.S. Navy photo by Public Affairs Officer Peter Walz)

With a fully dressed ship and streamers, U.S. Navy sailors assigned to USS Chosin (CG 65) man the rails as they await the pass and review in Sydney harbor. The crew is participating with 20 other global navies as part of the International Fleet Review - the 100th anniversary celebration of the Royal Australian Navy into Sydney. Chosin is currently operating in the 7th Fleet area of responsibility conducting exercises, port visits, and operations to enhance maritime partnerships and promote peace and stability in the Indo-Asia-Pacific region. (U.S. Navy photo by Public Affairs Officer Peter Walz)

U.S. Navy sailors assigned to USS Chosin (CG 65) prepare the anchor detail as they pull into Sydney harbor to join 40 other military ships and 17 historic tall ships as part of the International Fleet Review - the 100th anniversary celebration of the Royal Australian Navy into Sydney. Military forces from nearly 20 nations are participating in the events which will include public ship tours, fleet parade, and fireworks light show. Chosin is currently operating in the 7th Fleet area of responsibility conducting exercises, port visits, and operations to enhance maritime partnerships and promote peace and stability in the Indo-Asia-Pacific region. (U.S. Navy photo by Public Affairs Officer Peter Walz)

USS Chosin, a Ticonderoga-class guided-missile cruiser (CG 65), docks in the San Francisco Bay, Oct. 8, to take part in San Francisco Fleet Week 2014. The focus of fleet week is conducting interoperability training, enabling civil-military agencies and personnel to share techniques and procedures, which also gives them the opportunity to gain understanding of the roles, responsibilities and capabilities of each agency. (U.S. Marine Corps photo by Gunnery Sgt. Ajiboye Magbagbeola/Released)

APPENDIX 0. MOST VIEWED IMAGES ON DVIDS

USS Chosin, a Ticonderoga-class guided-missile cruiser (CG 65), docks in the San Francisco Bay, Oct. 8, to take part in San Francisco Fleet Week 2014. The focus of fleet week is conducting interoperability training, enabling civil-military agencies and personnel to share techniques and procedures, which also gives them the opportunity to gain understanding of the roles, responsibilities and capabilities of each agency. (U.S. Marine Corps photo by Gunnery Sgt. Ajiboye Magbagbeola/Released)

With a fully dressed ship and streamers, U.S. Navy sailors assigned to USS Chosin (CG 65) man the rails as they await the pass and review in Sydney harbor. The crew is participating with 20 other global navies as part of the International Fleet Review - the 100th anniversary celebration of the Royal Australian Navy into Sydney. Chosin is currently operating in the 7th Fleet area of responsibility conducting exercises, port visits, and operations to enhance maritime partnerships and promote peace and stability in the Indo-Asia-Pacific region. (U.S. Navy photo by Public Affairs Officer Peter Walz)

With a fully dressed ship and streamers, Chief Petty Officer Matt Mistove and other sailors assigned to USS Chosin (CG 65) man the rails as they await the pass and review in Sydney harbor. The crew is participating with 20 other global navies as part of the International Fleet Review - the 100th anniversary celebration of the Royal Australian Navy into Sydney. Chosin is currently operating in the 7th Fleet area of responsibility conducting exercises, port visits, and operations to enhance maritime partnerships and promote peace and stability in the Indo-Asia-Pacific region. (U.S. Navy photo by Public Affairs Officer Peter Walz)

Aboard the Japanese warship Makanami, Chief Petty Officer Matt Mistove and Lt. j.g. Kenneth Lee listen to and observe an Indonesian boarding officer as he briefs one of the boarding teams who participated in the exercise. U.S. Navy personnel from USS Chosin are participating in combined navies exercises and an International Fleet Review in Sydney Sept. 29 through Oct. 18. The fleet training exercise dubbed ADMM+, ASEAN Defense Ministers Meeting Plus, is a major multi-lateral activity to promote practical Maritime cooperation and information sharing among participating Indo-Asian-Pacific countries and to build a common understanding of interoperability procedures in maritime security matters. (U.S. Navy photo by Public Affairs Officer Peter Walz)

U.S. Navy sailor Lt. j.g. Kenneth Lee assigned to USS Chosin watches a boarding exercise between naval personnel from India and New Zealand. The fleet training exercise dubbed ADMM+, ASEAN Defense Ministers Meeting Plus, is a major multi-lateral activity to promote practical maritime cooperation and information sharing among participating Indo-Asian-Pacific countries and to build a common understanding of interoperability procedures in maritime security matters. U.S. Navy sailors assigned to USS Chosin are participating in combined navies exercises and an International Fleet Review in Sydney Sept. 29 through Oct. 18. (U.S. Navy photo by Public Affairs Officer Peter Walz)

www.ingramcontent.com/pod-product-compliance
Lightning Source LLC
Chambersburg PA
CBHW042009080426
42733CB00004B/48